Sublimity

Norfolk Poems

by Mary Gilonne

with brush sketches by Peter Norton

Sublime Norfolk Publishing

www.sublimenorfolk.co.uk

Cover photo, Peter Norton, Summer Sunrise -Wells-next-the-Sea

A CIP catalogue record for this book is available from the British Library
ISBN: 978-1-3999-5680-2

Published in 2023 by Sublime Norfolk Publishing

www.sublimenorfolk.co.uk

Printed by Barnwell Print Ltd., Aylsham, Norfolk NR11 6SU

Location of Places in Norfolk described in Poems

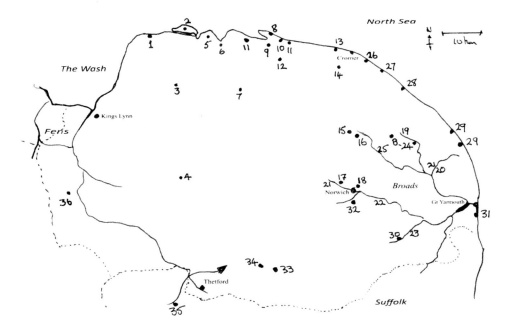

Contents

Foreword

Nowhere more embodies the essence of poetic emotion than Norfolk, a land that draws you in and holds you tight. There's something beautifully ancient and quietly apart about this county. Water, land, space, and a strange continuum of people anchoring time and place to something deeper than we can immediately comprehend.

When you walk these sublime expanses of coastal light, Holkham, Cley, Salthouse, the 'everyday' is reduced to insignificance. Here, our natural world is magnified to a quasi-spiritual dimension, tides and shifting sands that put us mortals in perspective. Marshland, salt and sky, this is a landscape of water-lines and a subtlety of colour so particular to Norfolk, nothing brash, all is in a brush-stroke palette of blues, greens, gold and sudden silver. Meditative and always uplifting.

The sea. What would we be without Norfolk's North Sea vastness, the clamour of its old herring fisheries, the dawn crabbers toiling out of Cromer, the distant ghosts of windmills turning the infinite horizon way way out. There's a continuous symbiosis of tradition and modernity that is so finely balanced here.

Wherever we turn our gaze, history beckons. Neolithic settlements, the ringing industry of flint pits, Boudicca rallying Iceni throngs. While, when standing on the green height of Mousehold Heath, the echoes of Norwich's past and present sound out in so many vibrations of change all around. The bloody tumult of Kett's Rebellion: the welcome of refugees, their looms weaving Tudor prosperity: the ebb and flow of 20th C household names…. yet all this renewal is rooted in an unequalled richness of the past.

So yes, Norfolk is sublime.

Mary Gilonne

Farmers, seamen
and labouring sails
swelling to the sea:
and on the wide plain
where the sand drinks
the briny ocean's spit,
my heart turned

I love the subtle worlds
weightless and charming,
worlds like soap-bubbles.
I like to see them, daubed
with sunlight and scarlet,
quiver, under a blue sky,
suddenly and burst…

from Selected Poems
by Antonio Machado
translation A.S.Kline,© 2004

Thomas Paine and Our Age of Unreason.

'I cannot accumulate when others have nothing.'

Now houses echo hollow in closed-door village
winters, lightless windows, a let of second-home
silence, rental high-water, never-ending moneyed
off-shore-swells, while he hand-threads still,
his sweated days with weaving waves of buff willow
and Flanders red, until the contained land curves
with his fielded fences which will outlive these drifting years.

'all land is the common property of the human race,'

His children's children become sand-banked further out
until their family buoy-line's lost. It's a land of new absences,
a sapping of old known walls, how each street he takes,
has forgotten its voices, the open gates of young
beginnings. How brick and mortar here, ghosts his days
and nights with impossibilities, how the desperate
erosion of displacement has the bloom and beauty of revolution.

*'landed monopoly has dispossessed more than half the inhabitants
of their natural inheritance, and has thereby created a species of
poverty and wretchedness that did not exist before'.*

*(Thomas Paine 1736-1809. 'The Age of Reason & The Rights of Man'.
Norfolk Political philosopher, he supported revolutionary causes in
France and America. 'Agrarian Justice' advocated that rich
landowners were dispossessing people of their natural inheritance.)*

1

And When I Remember This

there's eight year old me, a pink-ruched-cossie sea-slug, lying
on the surf-line. so much sky and sky
upside down trees in the clouds,
Holkham beach huts floating,
dunes of shifting light.

I never told you that cockles really sing. That with ear to pools,
down between tide-lapse and rising, very still,
I could hear their bright bubbled notes.
Nor that I knew the quick-tongue
names of pippits, dunlins,

how their feet skibbled the beach with deft Norfolk hieroglyphs
that only I could read. I never told you how far way out,
all that glass-bright sea seemed to pulse me
in landwards, how its edge-water lay
quiet like a settling bird.

I never told you that nightly from my window, jelly-fish glistened

tide-lines in a milky-way, nor how I longed to follow

cargo-ed horizons moving so darkly past. Strange

too how Winter's salt-spray finger-nailed

the gate with iced passings

as if our traces always show in certain slants of light without need of telling.

Now I follow stippled crab-walk sand-paths to hidden

marshes. Sea hungers in, eager for the coast,

so many high gulls wind-skimming,

simply searching like us

Watching Snow-Buntings in Cley.

Glasswort-green wetland,
smelted light. A tumble-flash
of boreal hiss.

Buntings feather-scape
sea's hinterland with white.
My lens flitters, clouds.

Air-fall confetties
in undulating chik-tik,
I'm cupped in calling,

lulled in a dune-quake
watching time and sky collapse
towards winging sleet.

Water links all this
to tidal creeks and marshes.
The birds silt-skim, settle.

Wind shifts saltly down
ruffling bird-foam, nest-scrapes dip,
bespeckled sand quiets.

Coast, marsh, paling mere.
I move through evening space
where I don't belong.

Rustles of keeled birds,
moon-leached shore, another place.
Homing like us all.

4

Watching Snow-Buntings in Cley

What is this North Sea Rain

bevelling wet morse flashes on my quiet window

                                   fast, fast

gorging gullies like alleys through tenements of torn

                                   grey grass,

fractured water casting saturations of frazzled willows,

                                   leaf-lines

water-falled. Loose pegged shirts in flight as if their wings

                                   earthbound

would beat in all this empty light, and then suddenly you

                                   night-less

phone from elsewhere. Some fickle bird breaks shadows

                                   hedges,

shifts from apple to plum. How I could hold its nesting bones

                                   crushed

in one cupped hand, how all my garden tows a weight of water,

                                   drowned.

Before

In this between day, we fold worry away like old thin napkins,
feign a serenity worn light as linen, try to lower our voices.

Your Aylsham garden never shadows till late, small talk adds up to
nothing. Waiting for illness to shrivel the apple of you to peel and core,

we tally the years in gold and dross, drink too much, too little.
dark makes us watchful as windows, and I know that each of us

is counting, gathering breath. August night hangs there, rustling,
dry as papery honesty, fragile silvered coins. Your sky is full of stars.

And Afterwards

How I pull open each dark drawer flowering dust to day.
Your pastels are in faded rows like piano keys,

thin tuneless sticks of hidden blanched hours, no tones
but those of the pith of lemons, powdered skin

or tinned pale salmon Sunday tea. I must pencil you in.
How your red coat hangs like a homing flag hooked fast

behind the kitchen door, pockets still full with your hands,
and the blue scumbled sky washed as it always was

with Norfolk flint and brick, slips down to the Bure.
I need to shade in your leaving, draw the curtains tight.

Dawn on the Cromer Ridge

How quickly my pulse leaves its hearth *full*. Pouched amadou,

        slip-quiver, time-feather fletch, taut yew bow, *again*

all chest-bound, tight once more. I'm this newly neolithic cliff-woman

high above a fast loping apex-line, as if coursing

        some ancient deer scutter, fibrillating rock *fall*

cutting sheer up, up through my winded breast of white.

halt   saccade   run

 a fleet youngling bolts light as forest fern

        furred lichen-soft flash rump and ashy stripe,

 hoof-cleaved *flight* of clay I count its blood-beat lead

be still   myself   breathe   gut-leap   ridge   rift-break,

a   crush   of   sudden   sky   sickles   thinning   light,

creviced   sun   shifts   seep-water   shadows   passing,

uneasy   gorse   gathers   night   birdcalls   darken   darkens

then   then   then

oh this beauty of a simple window waiting,

open again, rippling child-chatter, radio, kitchen thrum,

how mild my hunting heart returns tamed to me,

 lies quiet   *then oh then*

        recalls   your   *last-night* face   *land-slipped*   leaving.

Dawn on the Cromer Ridge

Day Job. (Bridge Street, Stiffkey)

He positions courses and laps along true regular lines.

Measures verge overhang, eaves-fall, top and ridge,

squares saw battens, strips, but-joints. Flashings, aprons

hips, the eroticism of roofing. Those nights full of loose

soughings, as if her quiet skin is leaving him, calls, slips.

Funny how a whispering sifts into his mind, grain by weather

blown grain, and that need to find broken bonds lays her absence

in ash-felt valleys. Almost primeval how toes clutch in his boots,

hanging on up here, tile ripper yowling and a fist of nails.

unbalanced now, bent against a hard ribbed sky. He hits the hammer,

twists shanks, slots old tingles. Climbing limb-feathered,

knuckle-bone pieces, red stacked counters, a pantile gamble.

How his drifting could be an easy fall of land. He's clay glazed,

face to wind, it blows the lie of her.

Flight.

Northern lights sheening down from the Wash.

I drop my bike, stone-quiet along an inky reed bed,

birds stippled, brushed above the river, ash-bled dye,

graphite dust. Rippling, pulsed with particle physics.

Thousands, a hiss of chittering sound in evening air,

all liquid, meshed. The ache of Winter, a gold flush

of leaves this morning when I cycled from you. Now

this bleed of redwings lifting light from furzed holts. Funnels,

folds, shape-shifting clouds weaved with fleeting songs

heard in Russia, Scandinavia. Birds sleeking the first colds

from their wings. later, when you and I realise what we've lost,

the Norfolk flats will freeze a little more, and beyond our rise

of woodland, still rime that feathered chissicking of invisible trees.

Planting Water

I'm up planting water on a marbled morning,
when tides have sifted, measured, leaving the dunes
salt heavy, and strung along the sucking edge
strands of bright gulls hanging slack, just drying.

Six bottles across the marsh of birds, plus shovel,
to this high point where Saturday we'll rig the tent.
The digging down, the acquiescent sand, soft
eddies and these sensual crushing shells. Life

is movement here, and promise. Sea-drifts build
the scape, pushing my lens to width and scope
and stretch the eye. My gift to you will be this lustrous light,
a well dark-damp, the bottles lying straight and true.

A final filling in, the levelled windy grains,
and then these flints to mark the spot, the source.
I know you'll laugh, *you did all this?* and archly sip
as if it's precious, which it is, my offering.

I'll dream up words, the weight, the time, better to plan

than carry burdens on the day. This creaming surf

will take us out and back and all could grow from here.

The hidden root of things, sea-thrift, sand-wort, samphire.

'Planting Water' was inspired by my brother's preparations for wild tenting on the North Norfolk coast, the carrying and burying of a water supply in the days before.

Homing.

Over the North Sea, clouds, like certainties, unravel with alarming force. Wherever my bus window turns, the sky's slipstream is full of sheared white fleece, a sudden bleached blue, then fat grey wind-eggs heavy with rain.

Arrival is like emerging from an armscye, a limb of ash and beech opens to flat green marshland, fingers of soft dykes draw my eye to a river, two red canoes scything the grass, and a waiting flinted house that never changes.

Sundays you used to phone, and there was always background birdsong, more poignant then than before when it filled our garden, tea in our hands, wisteria petals mauving everywhere. Now siskins and bramblings are chaffing hedges, a same path leads me.

All is intact. That old smell as if pears are ripening darkly still, the sigh of doors as I walk on through. I can feel you flickering in the frames of things, as if I'd never really closed your eyes. Indian rug, pegged sou'wester, good wine in the rack, a pleasure of photos

on whitewashed walls, gently weightless with old smiles and strings of days, framed bobbins and bibs, great-gran's collar-and-cuff artistry.

Lacemakers on gossiping quays, glass globes filled with sea- water and candle, working in that failing sepia light.

Later, there's a curlewed sky rising over the A11, full of bones, fragments of coast. My bus keeps track back to Stansted, queues of waiting cars are nothing more than gulls lined up along some Norfolk cliff, full of shadows. Landslides, gradual erosion, an uncertainty of home.

Mist in the Rabbit Hour

I'm this mute drifting valley unspooling Chet's river-lie
when you, flushed, unbuttoned, drunken homewards as dark

dies. My grey is a postscript under journeying clouds, a tumble
of shadows where hidden cows cud, and I temper the echoes of roads

with my wooling, your sign-posts and towns blank out, veer away.
I ghost hesitant pavements, mystify doorways, as you thread

through my wake in lamp-haloed *lokes,* and drink's nebulous names
are a mouthing of sounds when you search to recall who you slept

with last night. I chalk invisible birds in vague tattling trees and fletch
every leaf-line with feathers of light. Dawn whimples my vapours

around nunnish pubs, with clock-towers and pylons suspended in time.
Grass is spilt milk, I'm a delusion of hedges, regrets wraith Loddon Mill

with some hide-and-seek dance. You blanket yourself in my thankless
forgetting, I'm the point where paths end, where your nothing is chance.

('loke' is a lane)   15

That Year

in Blickling Park, Winter anglers weaved word-lines through fleeting
water and a man's heron-necked lamp fire-flied the dark

I folded myself in quiet, even trees never noticed the absence of me.

Seals breached an Autumn's Horsey gold, to birth in pure-blue tidal drifts
and a diver felt a heave of light beneath his fins

A wish-book of possibilities waited to be written and I did not, none.

In Castle-Acre's Spring, a child was taught the secret language of bells
and goats ruminated on the simplicity of things.

My hands hung heavy with the loss of others, I could not weigh their touch.

In Sheringham's bright Summer a woman loved in a sea of blossom, and
cat smiled in shadowed curl.

My pale room was drawn, bed-ridden, I could not let the morning clatter in.

In a seasonless shattered night, a Yemeni sat in a white corridor of dying,
naming each bright windowed star slowly, oh so very slowly. One by one.

That Year

The Ice House

You know it's there, unmissable, buttressing to innermost raftered dark,
    a lost theatre of silent spill within gault brick, seeping cold clear
        shadows through waiting slabs of light.

It's part of this East wind, heavying down in the slap and tar of old
herring sails, broad-keeled and dark. One-time, underneath fish sheds,
    water hauled its slump of weight while wharfs

tanged with ice-cart men hefting from ship to shore. Picture wakes of
    shoaling dockers, the crack of pack-ice, wherry-loads *dydled* on
        frost-hard dawns from down the winter's Norfolk Broads,

a hack and hew splitting air, hold your eye to the tides. How transient is
    life, like these ice-house walls abiding their chill timeless leach,
        you weigh the melt of things, your ever-fading place.

*(Built in 1840, the ice house at Great Yarmouth was used to store
ice brought down the river, first from the Broads and later from
Norway, it was used to preserve herrings which were then sent on to
Billingsgate. The ice house was crucial to Great Yarmouth's success
as a fishing port. Dydling – collecting ice off the Broads using a
large wire net, a dydle)*

18

Starling Sundown above Norwich

Chacker. This is sensory overload,
predator confusion, streets
carry them in night-lines,
underwings shrill
with city air.

They tip the shroud, hooding, fold
pleat. Swoop to plunder, scatter
cast among late gorging,
feathers slick as
night club knives.

Yellow rasps of beak, their shuttered eyes
will watch for cat-dust, death,
each neon breath of door,
churched hawks that fall
like endless stone.

They know our piss-cold dawns, guttered skies,
how forests of walls lock up
their light. Joyous blackness,
this pall of them
rising from the blocks.

The Sedge Cutter

threads along thin dykes,

his beamy *reedlighter*, shallowing through with shifts of quant,

cuddles banks and reeds,

while water thrimbles clinker in sucks and sighs.

He thinks of that summer night

when he came up past Hickling *roddon* in a rising *roke*

of stealing white,

dusk-sound simmering through the wet, his boat so heady

with *marsh litter* musk

that he had to drop his hands and let it drift.

The doe stood watching

from deep green *willow-carr,* flecks of pale along

her rump like a wake of stars.

How long he talked to her he doesn't know, but until a slur of orange-red

and a first bit of glowing

scythed down from the staithes. The doe slipped quiet, water curdled

him home with his *shoofs* of reeds,

and in the pub that night he never told a soul.

(Sedge and reed cutting is still very much a Norfolk Broad's activity, and is essential for thatching with local quality material. This poem was inspired by a young sedge cutter re-establishing a sedge marsh on the Ant opposite Irstead Green.)

Reedlighter - a shallow draft open boat used for transporting reed for thatching.
Marsh litter – a mixture of marsh plants.
Roddon – raised bed of a watercourse or tidal-creek
Roke – mist/ fog
Carr – a marshy woodland
Shoofs - sheaves

Timekeeping on the Marge.

You'll not find me here in this saturnine weight of pendulums,

        like his taciturn to and fro' our metered days counted

out at heavy pace and sombre chime, gaunt mantel-piece face

        witness to our coupled starts and stops to sit and

measure life's banal balances in a mahogany

        coffined case. Nor in the ormolu gilt of gran's *don't*

touch little tick and tock, which lives its vacuous days

        on the highest shelf glass-crazed by his

violent slip in turbulent times. Turn to the door and pause beside

        my clock of North Sea tides, its unhurried blue, that

single celestial hand. I'm the rise of water at every mystical lunar pull,

        I'm rhythmic seascapes of ebbing cloud

and setting coast. No key, no sound, only dried salt on the wind,

        a slippage of waiting sky, and me tiding otherwards.

'I want to live and feel all the shades, tones and variations of mental and physical experience possible in my life, and I am horribly limited'
Sylvia Plath.

Norfolk Alter Ego

a golden shovel after Sylvia Plath

In spite of night's old ghosts and vacant windows, or of anything he said, *I*
fill the room with flowers. Allium, foxglove, fleabane simply *want*
this quiet rhythm of purple repetition in homey water-jars *to*
calm a melancholic space. A door breathes brightness on the threshold, *Live*
this day it seems to say, nothing is displaced. I shrug a sweater on *and*
sudden outside air transforms to neon blue, trees froth with green, I *feel*
how sun-full is this confluence of now and then. Leaves, lop-sided hearts, *all*
hanging with intent to maybe drift or fall, stretch out to point some way. *The*
path turns, spilling gravel edges in a crunch of glee beneath my boots, *shades*
deepen to waves of indigo among the trees and dew-tippled grass. How *tones*
in his last night's voice fade so easily. Did he raise his hand or was it me, *and*
shadows did we shout, or do my thoughts just spin an axis on the *variations*
of a man? A frog like some leggy nut-cracker, tenses camouflaged pretence *of*
bided time before the coming leap. Its culvert slimes with spawn, and *mental*
images of childhood tapioca swim milky comforting, some ghosted light *and*
otherness I catch from way back when. Picture him, a Worsted giant, *physical*
vocality, the brilliant alchemy that led us to all this, our slow walk, *experience*
of words budburst shrapnel on flint walls, as if our wars were always *possible*
even then. When I feel kitchen flagstones hold morning cold beneath my feet *in*
early hours, when thoughts are brackish marsh water thinning over stones, *my*
pen clasps tight. You can recognise fieldmice by listening to their running, *life*
patters on short paths, I guess I do too. It's strange how my urgencies *and*
yearnings return faithfully as North Sea tides, and in his bright reflected water *I*
drown a little more. I *am*
knowingly, *horribly*
limited

Balloons.

On the day I nearly left our future,
it was in a wicker basket on ascending currents,
breath tipped with trees, looking down and away.

Morning had seen me dressing, edgy as an insect,
a fleeting reflection of wings multiplied in mirrors,
trying to hold back flight, abandon thinning bedroom air.

We'd billowed out from Earlham, tongue-tense, autumn
blight browning fields and both of us full of louring sky.
Grapes of balloons rose slow, like rainbow bursts toward the sea.

Lifting. I believed leaving could be as simple as this, almost
an easy sigh of slipping land. How to explain that sudden shift
of light, the necessary weight of you, how close I came to falling?

Balloons

'Our lives are the lines missing from the fragments' Selby Wynn Schwartz

Aground.

I'm walking on a grassy sea of rise and fall,
birds trailing masts of trees like scattered smoke.

This river abrades its unfolding, it torques away
from a timeline of old banks, while down in the dark tea

of peat-pickle, a boat simply sublimes its rudderless voyage
as if everything above has no hold. A lych-gate of roots rigging

deep earth, scarfed strakes, pegs and tar, dims of little things that trace.
I can almost hear the underlie, how rope-tow groaned oak timbers

in their docking, loose knots of voice around haggled withy creels of catch.
Now invisible people are only vibrations in this Norfolk air. How our imprints

will always leave these journeying parch-marks, all the lost keels and rivets
of life we cast behind. Why we're always searching for what we cannot see.

*(In 2013 a medieval, boat dating back to 1400, was unearthed along the River
Chet near Loddon during construction of a drainage project. It was a rare and
important find, no other medieval boats have been discovered in the region. It
would have had a sail, and been used to ply goods back and forth to markets
along the lakes and waterways of the Broads.)*

Norfolk. Haiku Seascapes.

Silt-wash of bird runes.
A throating of gull-spelt air
salt words on my tongue.

Early sharpened sky.
Horizons thinning northwards
a whet of steel-grey.

Evening harvest.
Coracles of *stewkey blues.*
Suddenly plovers.

Setting night-water.
A blush of translucent drift.
Moon jellyfish glow.

Sea-sheen beaching up.
Filigree of morning kelp
Gilded cormorants.

Salt-marsh tidal pool
Fish-eye aperture of blue
Lug-worm hinterland.

(stewkey blues : small blueish cockles from Stiffkey.)

'May you enter favoured and leave beloved.' Ancient Egyptian Prayer.

Hathor.

Night jars churring.

Ibis white as gypsum feathering our Nile, my last drawn breath flowed with
pale shadows fleeting me.

My skin is lily, myrrh.

Limbs smooth as sandalwood and on my linen-ed breast a mewing kitten
milkied with the loss of me.

This was my horizon.

Reeds, purple valley, arms, delta, eyes, love's quiet ear a whorl of sepals,
chalice. Women with-out me.

Red kites, red Saqqara.

Oh for water pleating through green palms to slake my mouth of sand and
stone. River within me.

How hands hush now.

Sweet attar, argan, musk, lighten my serene limbs to youthful nudity. White
lotus wreathes along me.

28

They scribe my life.

What a dear ravishing thing is immortal light, walls stippled sepulchred

gold. Safflower blushes me.

Air has no weight,

swaddled in eternal clouds, my future carved above in a Book of Sky, Day,

Night. May *Ka* sail with me.

(*The unique Norfolk Wherry* **'Hathor'**, *was named after the Egyptian
Goddess of love, beauty, fertility and pleasure. Alan Colman, young son of
the famous Norfolk Colman Mustard dynasty, died on the Nile near Luxor
in 1897 from tuberculosis, and his heartbroken sisters had the boat built in
his memory in 1905. The lavish, remarkable interior was designed by the
architect E.T. Boardman, and its serpent-head lamps, teak marquetry of
lotus flowers and animals, is based on Egyptian hieroglyphics and
mythology.* **'The Hathor'** *is preserved by the Wherry Trust, and is still used
for scheduled sailings.)*

Last Pub Standing

These King Street shadows.
On unmoored nights when the Wensum slips, you might hear still
the wraith of one Tom Bates, drunk as a natterjack in The Nag's Head,

'four days haul 'bro in rafty weather, from Horsey Mere to Thurne
my old Black Sail quanting calm, and the excise men coming up the Bure'

as fifty-eight tavern doors yawn out in spill and shout, eddies of wherrymen
in raucous wakes of bootleg rum. He's oiled as an eel in gansey and tars,

'there were Tall Mill sails stopped at ten-to-four, and old miller signals
up in his window-watch, so we slowed us down before Womack Water'

and his face ruddies up with tales of the chase, Nag's black cellars stack
his contraband casks, and grey brewers-drays clatter hooves in the Street

'and the cockey was deep with squalling rain, so we dumped all our kegs
by a hansers lie, and the excise upped off towards Hickling way'

while he counts his shillings on the wood of the bar as the publican
leans with a fourth rum jar, mid the rollicking press of mawthers and men,

'and the marshman pumped till our kegs were dry, and we scarpered up the
Yare in a furrow-chuck's flash. Our rum is best your money can buy!'

and Tom Bates falls down on the Nag's flag floor, dead as the dark in
river's deep, his rum-run gains in the palm of a *fern*. King Street shadows.

(The Last Pub Standing- The Nag's Head in 1840 - is the only pub left of
the 58 that were in King Street. King Street is parallel to the main port of
Norwich. Smugglers coming up from the Norfolk coast supplied the taverns
with contraband rum.)

rafty - cold and damp; cockey – dyke; hanser - heron
mawthers – girls and women; fern – prostitute.

Night Scene

She is pond apple, cypress-swamp,

in this dim other-land of Englishness.

If I shine a torch she will appear mothed,

frayed white, framed by door, glass, step,

a photographic negative of sleeping woman,

bag and wall. Rare in these Norwich streets,

exotic as ghost-orchids, mangroves, war.

She's lapped by blooms of plastic black,

like bursts of waterlilies by her side. Lamped,

the plaited shadow of her hair un-prints

each pillowed paper page, her written cheek.

How night blurs, leaches those neon details

of her day, its deprivation of sky, guttered birds.

My reflected hand hangs, I'm spinning mirrors.

Day Trip to a Distant Edge. The Watch House.

Everything here is further than the moon,

this house minds its rarity of air in little things.

Boxed memories, inner emigrants.

I sew pieces of reality back to back,

the stuff of families, frayed facts,

darned and underpinned, unpicking old threads.

Look that hand-bagged rectitude of granny's posture,

hands cool as pious fish, a brown steady flow

of knick-knacked parlour tea, blanched widowing.

Brothers pegged and door-slammed, fitful, fistful,

taut as washing lines. Mum, sweetly starched,

bleached by all she never chose to see,

and Dad, bricked, claggy with our mortar,

building us in. Home is a far dying star,

planetary nebula, such a distant constellation.

Day Trip to a Distant Edge

Bloodgate.

Sit quiet.

There's a needling strain of light stitching this disappearing place,

ancient space girdled with faint encircling. Today's sheep, speck

almost symmetrically the grassy inner ring, Burn Valley folds its green,

as the North Sea gentles air with a salted wind. A kestrel threads your eye,

lifting the pause, the lull, the blue between. Sudden, you catch a sear

on ebbing air, some ancient memory set on fire, charcoaled hearths, squalls

of children, cries. Palisades roundel with chanted rituals, rites, watchers

deciphering, falling dark, eras collapse, ramparts rise, then in a stabble of

roily mud a primal bare-footing of live-stock, men, wraith out of your

seeing. Holm oaks root down, hazel hedge confines. This anonymous field

spreads out its turf and rests above much deeper lives. Far off traffic filters

through your day, southerly clouds build a chance of coming rain. We all

carry still this age-old weight of things.

Sit quiet.

*(Blood gate Hill is an important example of an Iron Age Fort, it lies near
South Creake, Norfolk. Its use is uncertain, ceremonial, refuge from raids
and skirmishes, a dramatically situated gathering place? It remains a site
of atmospheric beauty)*

Contorted Drift. East Runton.

She's drowning in-between, in being there and here
like cliff-fall and sea. Whales loom in hotel corners,
watch her smoothing pillows, sheets, with a sonar-ed
clicketing of tongues. Tell how winter moonlight pools
zooplankton, liquid dust, as she polishes each mirrored
ripple. Tidal tales of loss and harpooned solitude.

When he left, she read that dolphins grieve,
cling to a floating line of sea and sky for days.
She pictures his skin swimming in tiled shadows,
an elvering of water, those shoulders softly rilled.
Wonders if infidelity spawns here too in every passing
 room she cleans, invisible as a ritual of eels.

She's slipping underneath, holds on to absent walls.
Pebbles of voices purl from bedded lives, as if each
glassy shallow, teems with the little fish of things,
morning's flotsam regular as tides. Driftwood hours,
her hands are palmed with the counting. She's sea-cave,
shell, the North Sea wave of him has washed right through her.

Dew Pond. Remembering a Forgotten Landscape.

Water shrinks. Imagine how Summer droughts its way to Winter thinning
as dew ponds sap, and early chill nuzzles lambing grass with thirst. The
hollow waits for brume. This moist-dark bowl, mud-wort rimmed and wide

gasps for Spring when the *gangers* come shirt-sleeved and loud to puddle
clay, to shovel out more stark-white pans of chalk, mat-down wiry osiers.
Sheep scrag round in unbothered clots of grazing cream along the furze,

as if the clangour of dogs and spades is no less seasonal than shears
before some Worsted Fair. Each village, farm, cups in its midst a want of
water. Every sky-pooled eye, transient as moonshine, bides a misting
dawn-fill wet.

It's strange this business of time, how the silted fades in Norfolk fields
and copse, circle their dips with ancient water-lines that mark old ghosts of
man and flock. I walk dew-drunk grass in search of something lost.

A dragon-fly hovers, fluid blue.

*(Dew ponds, ghost-ponds, mist-ponds. Norfolk holds more ponds than any
other English county… over 23,000. Most were located on farmland and
were essential livestock watering ponds dug in the 17th and 19th centuries,
or had their origins in clay or marl pits. Many have disappeared but their
traces remain.*
Gangers= itinerant labourers)

Dew Pond

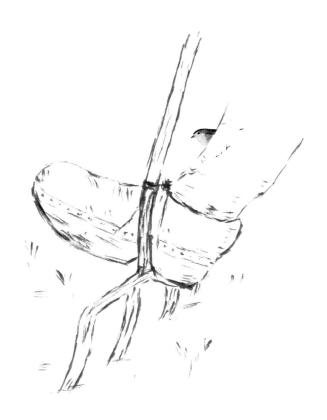

I Dream of Fen Skaters

they come up through the meadow's flood and freeze, to where grass
meets ice. Their cloud-lands stretching straight as a die along dykes,
drains, cuts, thin the horizon down to Welney in frigid greys and tacks

of long-stitched trees. You told me yesterday of 1855, that it's *Pattens* first,
old *fen-runners* beech-wood nailed. That booted they skitter the edge in
nicks and ice-dust crosses, waiting for the start. The race is on, it's cold it's

fast. One mile to the frozen flag and back, the high-pitched shrilling of their
blades sifting my ears like widgeon whistling the wind. *Turkey Smart* folds,
doubles down head-to-knees, pares the water-glaze as if his speed is

nothing more than a sparrowhawk's shearing down the course. The crowd
frost-banked, bets and cries, victory mutton hangs outside the pub, and as
the brass band trumpets '*Cheer boys, cheer',* he cuts the barrel-turn in

sparks of glassy ice and fastens up along the levee to break that final line. I
can almost see his breath shimmer, as boggy boots untied he yokes his
shoulders with the sharps as if carrying the lightness of a winter's day.

When I open my eyes, your morning arms will shawl my neck in just this

way, and our window will frame the Fens as always in their slip of braided

marsh right out to Welney Washes and the sky. You'll turn and tell me how

clouds of lapwing lift in the red of dawning sun, how teal flock in on

easterly winds along wetlands' shine, that you'll take me there before

the coming thaw to hear swans mewling overhead. My cool hands skate,

your skin is taut and smooth as glass, gliding is easy, I'll never fall.

*(Fen skating dates from medieval times, and by the 19th century had
become a feature of cold winters. For agricultural workers, competitive
speed skating added to their winter income. Shallow water in fields and
marshy land iced over more quickly than on flowing water and was safer.*

In the Fens, skates were called **pattens** *or* **fen-runners. William 'Turkey'
Smart** *(1830-1919) was a farmworker and champion speed skater, whose
reign began in the Fens in North Norfolk at Welney. One of the greatest
Fen skaters of all time, and races attracted thousands of spectators from
far and wide)*

Ten Years On

and I'm moled down again, quiet in an under-bank rut of fissling reed
watching sky murmurate the Broads with something more than inky wings.
The comfort of earth, its scrabbled dank, bones of my precious things
hidden a little deeper every year. I can almost see you still, a watery need

ghosting this river along wherry paths, old dykes, though blindness is a
bleed of shadow that slips between my now and then. It's strange how
mud-rings worm their way in never ending circles here, all that underlife
simply brings the thought that if I dig and dig I'll find you as you were.

All tunnels lead to light, a place to breathe, my nails are claggy with the
trying. I read once that moles grabble their solitary lives with a quiet
purposefulness, picture hidden paths labyrinthing every root and stone.
My inner ear vibrates with insect tread, a scurry of tracks and fear

with every trespassing shift I take, their pit-pat dread of unknown things.
Now there's lustrous pelts of water-light across leaf-scatter, and I burrow
into another day. The constancy of traces, nothing is really dead.

Ten Years On

Apples.

It wasn't that you ran to the Bure
as women might do, back to the birth,
the breaking of the waters.
It wasn't that I could picture you, thin
and urgent as a mayfly.
It was the choice of day, when all was
pregnant with light and promise,
and I was gathering apples in
your soft shawl.

I didn't see the old spent boat and you,
floating frail. I didn't hear
the ripples repeat, repeat, tattling back
to tell. I didn't hear you murmur
time is ripe and smile at
shadowing shades. I was laying apples
warm on yellow plaid, thinking
of your bright face before the blanching
of your mind.

I hadn't left you long alone, too long
as longing is. I hadn't seen the river
flowers, blue speedwell wet about
your eyes. I hadn't thought that space
could be as white as skin to touch.
It was that time of day,
when all was taut with now and then,
and I was harvesting apples
in heedless hands.

Pumpkin Chant, Thursford.

Come down to where these buttocky buoys
mark out in docile rows a shifting sea
of wind-lashed hedge.

Come to the laboured limits of your farm,
its waves and troughs boot deep, wallow
in butternuts.

Come past blank gardens, polyphonic blacks,
forget the stars or gesturing night-noised trees,
covet my curves.

Come touch this earth-silked orange skin,
sleek and gently grooved for harvesting hands, heavy
as milky breasts.

Come follow my glow like an autumned moth,
you sowed your seed on a faithless dawn, now reap.
I'm pregnant with light.

Happisburgh.

Storm surge, erosion, a relentless abiding tiding-out , this coast

retreats in burials and unearthings. Look. Fifty footprints walk

upstream, kin and clan, soles miring in the quag. Gatherers, crab, kelp,

lugworms, shells, scavenging the flow. Pine and birch, grassy heath,

their river valley mammoth grazed, puddled with brackish pools,

they potter, pause, squelch heel-arch-toes, each trace embedding

clag-stiff silt. A strong North-Wester lifts, the rushing water-course

diverts and scours in timeless repetition, their footmarks scutter on.

Now one million years from them, these onshore winds still plunder, sea

gnaws in and toothless groynes, steel, greenheart, jarrah wood, surrender

to an ever-moving beach, this soft geology of edges. Stoic, high fields

fresh-drilled with wheat, vanish in night's block-fall, while round cliff's

tumbled underlie, running sand sludges, mudflows gully, boulder clay

slumps. How this hinterland recedes apace, the red-white lighthouse

encroaches on the marge, while wayward footpaths accelerate their fall and

plummet to the sea before our eyes. Loss, demise. Once fifty footprints

walked, within two weeks the lives they held had washed away.

(In 2013 a set of hominid footprints were discovered in uncovered sediment on Happisburgh beach. They are the oldest known hominid footprints outside Africa, and date to 1,000,000 years ago when Happisburgh lay about 24 kms inland at the site of the estuary/maritime bay of the ancestral river Thames.

Tidal erosion meant that researchers had little time to document the find, and the footprints were destroyed by the elements. Happisburgh is faced with the worst coastal erosion in the UK, losing land and houses at an unstoppable rate. Climate change, sea-rise and the increased frequency of extreme weather are accelerating the phenomenon).

This poem relates to the traditional art of embroidery in Norfolk cloth manufacture.

Crewelwork in Times of Loss

My fingers blight   mothing shades

    our old knots   shuckle light

       miss-budded   canvas daguerreotype

           time overripe

Needle pricking   pale cross-rhythm

    pass-under-drop-two   wool spools me

       stuttered leaves   lint-grey sheep

        grazing welts of green

Snagged sky trips   my slip-stitch

    fades this pounce line   clouds hand tightens

       taut jute hooping   her indelible overlay

        printed through you

Red madder cutch lye   such bitter couch-work

    these stalks sap   biling dye's leach

       a flowered canker   founders my last thread

          before

          I

         cut.

On Finding the Photo

The foreground is enough to know,
flowers brash warning lights and him
in black and white, stopped, waiting for the flash.
Photos lie. The woman there still life, hands
semaphoring back across a puzzled beach.
Her eyes are shaded by a silly hat
and the grey air stretched with a drumming pause.
Look at the edge, their sand-shoed feet in line
with stones and grass, a blur of blue as if
she'd moved. The bold gull outline of her lips,
driftwood by her knee, a parted dress.
he's heard the click and smiles in time. Steps back
is caught and framed before the act is thought.
Observe the clues. That brassy gorse will do,
you need no more to set the scene. But glance
towards the shadowed left, a picnic plaid,
the glint of knives, a radio. His head
half-turned, temple veined, an unshaved pulse.
Photos lie. They draw you in to what you
want to see. The courage is to look beyond.
A breathless flight towards the surf, then up
a smothered line of sight to Holkham's roofs.
A smudge of dunes, a quivering cry of air.

Stranger

Smoke over my Low Countries, burning *religie* and flesh,

laments of wrested books and *hopeloos* souls. Heretic.

Leaving was such a bitter North Sea flounder,

hearts branded with fire, salt and loss.

Then this long cantering coast bright as belief,

and now I'm here, wife and *kinderen. Protectie, protectie*

within Norwich's flinted walls. *Dank u wel* for the sanctuary

of otherness, for your pale delft washed skies that weft *godshuis*

with weavering light, these soaring workshop windows

shuttling English clouds, and the Wensum shimmering

like my river Scheide , all slipped with threaded dark.

How our chackering looms treadle place and words in shedded wool,

how my hands brim with *bombazine* and *dorneck* stuffs.

Tallow gloams my past with shadows, may it illumine all I have to come.

(In 1565, 30 Dutchmen and their households, Protestant refugees seeking asylum from persecution in the Catholic Low Countries, found sanctuary in Norwich encouraged by Elisabeth 1ˢᵗ.

The 'Strangers' as they came to be known, were master weavers and revitalised not only the 'New Draperies' of the textile trade and made Norwich its flourishing centre, but also enriched the local community.) bombazine – a cloth made of worsted weft and silk; dorneck – a silk and wool twist in invisible stripes.)

Stranger

Sonnet for a Poet

Your burial in another era would have flamed across a thundering fjord.

I'd have nested you in a deer-skin coracle, wassailed on gold-lit mead,

scattered *millefiori* around your linen shroud, or sealed a cryptic hoard

of runes in some honeyed oak-wood vat. It's hard to follow our journey's lead

today, sky hangs pewter-heavy in this Norfolk town, and along our garden path

we're only two, you asleep in willow, me on foot in grey. Cars pass untroubled

by the knowledge that you're gone, dogs bark, kids shout, you'd laugh

to hear how even the factory sirens blast the clouds, as pubgoers huddled

before opening in pouring rain, curse the minutes on the church clock-tower.

I remember how near Quidenham you heard a goat-horn through a stand

of trees and said it called for you, that your days were counted but the power

of words would see you richly through, that sagas are as sonorous as this land

that buries us. Now stations fill with people, buses redden arteries of rush hour

streets, a door is closed. Somewhere Valhalla opens, all of this you planned.

The Knot Collector in Wells-next-the-Sea.

He handles rope with a lover's care,
hours coil out with oiled manila,
sisal twists, twines of hay-sniff hemp,
flax-ed, frayed in chandler drawers
waiting to be hitched and spliced,
fingers neat as needles, purled.

He's mastered all the ins and outs,
sheet-bend, sheep-clove, double -loop.
Berthed and cleated imaginary yachts
moored in every coir or juted port,
belayed his nights with alpine-butterflies,
abseiled nirvanas through sleep-blind snow.

He diaries life in Inca cords, bedroom quipu
code quiet walls with strings of secrecy,
girls are lonely abacus in passing nodes
of red or blue, a tallying of fingered threads.
One day soon he'll noose a gallows knot,
there's enough sweet slack to hang himself.

Sea-henge

We sunk this mortuary of roots under a cold sky spreading,

split fifty-five stakes to circle one in that late oak Spring,

bronze-fisted and willing.

Sopped turf swallowed timbers in a throng of night chants,

and our axes cuffed salt air with a dulling thrum,

harsh shrub, soft marsh.

Now this woman I used to lie with, hides a tiny shell in her ear,

white as cuckoo flowers, furrows peat-dark clag along

her deadened skin,

every wish-bone runed with black. A body's offering,

dark sea-birds in the offing, and my pale-mooned kin lean

as if divining a new light.

Talons will tear, bloody beaks rip, yet skulls stay taut as

resonant drums. In Winter's thinness she'll fall in fertile rain

but oh, oh my barren loss.

*(In 1998 on a beach at Holme-next-the sea, a 4000 year old Bronze Age
timber circle was discovered. A huge tree stump with roots uppermost, and
55 oak-wood posts around it.*

*Originally on fresh-water wetland, erosion and tidal surge had changed the
landscape and it had become sea-bound. It was concluded that the ancient
henge and inverted stump were used for ritual and excarnation, i.e. 'sky
burial')*

Sea Henge

Aylsham Day Care.

Pavements here are earth, quiet water, sky.
We push up slow through last night's wet,
runneled wakes of grass wheel back behind each muddy step.
Poodled trees, pollarded to fluffs of leaf, lean spindled limbs,
lead on to low flint buildings, careful shoulderings
of hedge that pass, contour, contain.

This is shawled land, she wraps it round her tight.
A winding-sheet of path, wide forgetful windows
searching clouds as if glassed days are somehow lost
behind clipped privet lines or nunnish lily stems;
while dark doors stand, full of tepid tea and waiting.
We're sensitive as chameleons to all this in-between.
Know life is neither here nor there, like estuaries and sea.

Rococo in Banham Zoological Gardens.

A mardi gras of parakeets bicker gaily as I wander,
paper bags of grain, a pudgy toddler hand in mine,
aiming unsteadily for a creamy-cupped magnolia.

Within its glossy leaves, two peach-faced lovebirds
catch the aviary windowed light and I think of Fragonard,
'The Swing', a distant summer at the Louvre, an age away

from North Sea skies. How that playful painting, intimate as you
and me in our beginnings, held us fixed while half the world
passed by. Loose, florid, that ballet-pink dress lapping silken out

like some hot-house flower, the paramour's curved arm, an arboreal
shimmer. How we both, lounging by the Seine, waxed drunkenly lyrical
on Fragonard's frantic dog, the two complicit putti, and in spite of all

the painting's mirth and joy, how that cuckolded husband in crepuscular
shadows watched the coming of the end of things. Now two *inseparables*
tilt and sway, eyes half closed, the bright mica of their beaks blinking

in the tree. Toddler scatters seeds by handfuls like Cromer sand, wings
fly down in a candy-coloured carefree chittering while Banham sky pools
its blue in coursing clouds, a blue deep enough for me to drown in,

Advice from a Ladder Encountered on a Cromer Street Corner.

1/

Avoid casual triangular affairs, they religiously end with a fist of nails,

remember you have a sombre ancestral relationship with gallows.

Do not overshadow passing mortals with your fixed trinity of views,

beware the ostracism between wall and air, that head-in-clouds *troshel* slip.

2/

Never lean too far in the pursuit of otherness. Imagine Salthouse herons,

their graceful pin-point poise, neither obtuse in their trying nor over-reached,

or the acute perceptive *v* of flying geese, how its angled compass simply is.

Beware though pissing dogs, sly cocked legs, it is all to easy to lose your feet.

3/

Your rungs are your rank, the higher you climb *St Peter's and Paul's* greater

the vista, but do not let this go to your head, you're only as tall as your last

stretch, and grounded you are nothing more than a hopscotch path for children.

All is in the being, never be tempted by a pretence of coastal curves and turns.

4/.

Always be mindful that you are an extension of others, yet your still-life

is far more than North Sea skies, a *mawkin's* stance, rough hauls of hands

or sea-gull droppings. Recollect that Jacob dreamt you, that O'Keefe took

you to the moon, that your raison d'être between here and heaven is ascension.

(Norfolk dialect: troshel – doorstep, mawkin – scarecrow)

Advice from a Ladder,

Encountered on a Cromer Street Corner

Ana, Afhak, Filipa, Bruna. A Migration of Seasons.

When we arrived
I learnt how hard it was to measure the weight of walls
and stranger stones.
How settling was mapped with the latitudes and contours
of everyone, but us.
How foreign words were like shells, hinged so tight they could
only whisper sea.
How we carried quiet ghost ships harbouring spaces,
preparing, preparing.
How we were beached by the ebb and flow of otherness,
trying to simply float.

When we stayed
I learnt that we have the hidden force of generations
of solitary travellers.
That the arms of prehistoric women were stronger
than modern rowers.
That the tides of learning have us navigating by touch,
light so often lost.
That working is a quest for becoming, frontiers are made
to be crossed.
That all you think you leave behind is never there, time
sifts people, places.

When we remembered

I learnt how landscapes write our language, how easy it is
to translate eyes.

How a dreaming daughter is forever imagining, echoing old
perfect pictures.

How language is a birthing/berthing, that words are place,
havens, wombs.

How sudden sloping light can hologram any Norfolk field with
our abandoned South.

How a *Where're you from mawther?* has me picking figs and olives
on some distant moon.

Oncology for Beginners in Norfolk and Norwich University Hospital.

Today new words **fish** our mouths in this patient watershed, and we learn
to read a compass. Biological maps and files, dense with jungled tissue,
lymph and bone, lie open on her desk. Her nails, pink as orchid petals,
search hidden corners for the distant humming-birds that **seed** this
gorged blooming in you, an exoticism of some unknown growing. Our
boundaries are door, white noiseless corridor, a windowed corner of bird-
eyed blue, and on her wall a photo of a greening canopy that seems to
sanctify this air with scent. You strip down, layered flat, palely leafed. She
fits a lisping snake of lasered light to fit, then calls you to the tunnel, an
explorer in a precisely minuted desert **night**. Egg-timer, hour-glass, our
eyes rake each other's for that **lost**   **lost** grain of sand. It's strange
how later **silence** makes us garrulous, how we're white-watered now with
rushing plans **to do**   **to love**   **to be**   **to love**. Outside, a Norwich sun
juices flint walls like ripe Maracuya, pavements are a flush and fluster of
scarlet blossom drifting in from some far   **unknown**, and we wander
wide-eyed through flesh-soft red like visitors to another land. **Later**
later   she had said after the journey, **later**   **later** and I **translate**
translate   how an ocean of **quietude** **quietude**   will pulse all your
frontiers, how beams of energy **glow**   **glow**   in dark, how she will
mould invisible geography into a newly chartered piece of **you** **you**
you. Bishop's Bridge is strong as a wishbone beneath my feet,

on borrowed **light** now

a glide of gull-throated **air**

flares some sea with **sound.**

Oncology for Beginners in Norfolk and Norwich University Hospital.

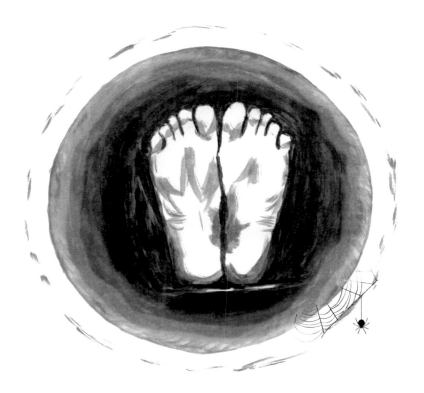

Riverbank Rhapsody.

Listen how this River Ant willow is greenly strung and boughed,
An essence of cello in the blue, and like some leitmotif in reflected skies
it plays the water in connecting notes. Skin is shimmer, Lily's troutling thighs
dip, rippling our shallows with four-year-old glee. And when the music's loud
enough to catch the sound of oboes slendering sinuous ways among the cloud
of reeds to oscillate in rhythmic bright, she tries to capture passing mayflies
in her chubby hands and puddle-stamp a timpani of falling leaves as it plies
its way on down towards the Staithes. Forget the town, its noisy overcrowd
of jangling sound. Picture red-sailed wherries maundering through the Broads,
constancies of river-bank mills, all is movement, flow, nothing is improvised,
not this resonance of liquid shine nor harp nor strings. We're neither here
nor there, the orchestra swells, the Ant drifts, dilates in trills, whorls. Chords
of light pick out our flinted house in rusts and greys, a passing thrush surprised
by melody hops near. Norfolk rests, Lily pebbles toes. We live another year.

The Play of Sun on a Prospective Lover.
Scolt Head Island.

Today, I'm building a quiet mandala of you,

limbs open gates, your body sand. A drifting

east and west of space, down here where wind

breathes water, and sea kelp billows greenly far

far out, borrowing light from all this burning blue.

Dunlins dip, turning stones of sound like time-pieces,

counting the edging tide as it lips along your skin

in ways I've yet to learn to do. I could leave us here.

You star-circled, washed, transparent as a saint,

and me kneeling, a meditative colourist in shifting shells.

I am a gull's distant eye, I magnify our little things.

The winged shadow of my arm, your conched hands,

how sea holds a sliver of sky from a mackerel flank,

the way sun fishers me in, hesitant as baited water.

Gansey

Oh I'm casting my man out of water and wind,
purling dark sea from a worsted of blue, through a
needling and sailing of skeins 'cross my lap
as the crabbers dawn-out in patterns of sky.

Past shuttering channels to shanks of corked pots,
he's out weaving the sea in his gansey and slops,
and I nimble my waiting, splice out my yarn, praying
for landing, full crinnies and calm. Oh that aching of clinker,

bloodying bait, how the race thunders in as I worry my wait
while dusk's indigoed drift ebbs and plies through my wool,
marking cables and lines with a coiling of spool, the slack

that runs with each fishering stitch will be roped by his oaring,
salted and wracked. Oh I'm boding us fair in this gull-throated light,
may the harsh rime of his face be bed-sweetened tonight.

Gansey

Kittywitch Row.

slat as a fish-barrow
        sour nose to tail,
              hip-broad,
                   fingers follow night
            east to west
       herring-ed in tight,
     lamp-shine shoaling walls
 down port up quay,
        brazen bedlams
          scavenger gulls
              shirted breasts loose,
         bloody faces soused,
      trawling hard coin
    a bawdy of liquored
longshore sharks.
      Caulk your ears littl'uns
         whilst all of a
             muck-wash, mariners
       tide our bone-thin
 Row, kitty witched
        by clinker bait
          guttered with cobbled hauling.

(kitwijk – the Dutch for house of ill repute, e.g.Kittywitch Alley in Great Yarmouth. From medieval times, 'low' women trooped from house to house during herring fairs, demanding money, dressed in men's shirts and their faces smeared with blood.)

Horizon Blakeney North Sea.

Here is no pale clemency. Do not be lulled by this calm
curving limb of consenting sand, nor the gentle tidal glow
reeling in its bycatch of salt-finned clouds. Read the air.

Do not believe the ghostly semaphored gestures of sea-mills
gathering wind, nor the silent shears of dutch sails cutting
to the Wash. Simply notice now, how far off margins shrill

with gulling. Look past the far waiting blaze of sand-bars,
past oystering birds like clips of quartz in the slippage
turning a glitter of unladen shells with their anglings of white.

How this relentless rote of sky scours out our scar of coastal
days until liberation, that final sigh of open water. How we stand forever
cleaved between restless sea and land, constantly fording the drift.

Fish-wharf.

A whole shoal of us lassies toil up along curing-yard,
and sailors all fish-eyed with our sweet darling songs,

pull dozens of creels, caulked kegs brim to the gills
with their night-sousing catch, while the salt-silvered flicks

of our slit-quick knives, gut herrings and men with the lust of our hands.
How the farlin-troughs roil with this autumn's trawl as the drifters

moor up and holler their haul, and we girls cloot our fingers
with cloth wedding rings and yell at the smart of salt-wounded stings,

muddying our blood with offal and bone. How our skin is a stitching
 nicked channels and bars, how the rime in our hair has the smell of this sea

when a man runs his hands through each current and wave. My dear Orkney
love is codding up off the Faroes, an eking of time, taut-water away,

while here akimbo slaving for pennies, oiled slick like a bloater, scabbed
with these fish-scales, how I long for fresh linen, his arms and my Tay.

Fishwharf

That Last Day

found me lip-reading the sea from my Gorleston window,
trying to make out its sprint of gleaming dashes
some sort of illegible morse drifting in from the north.

Usually here, there's a soundscape of high birds and lapping
coast, never those strange bass organ-chords grinding, a deep
underscore lamenting through the bight.

But then it was the first day, only 24 hours after he'd left.

Light was passing as if through silver-coated plate, changing
my stone-washed walls to shifting shadows. A few people
were frozen negatives on the strand, heads turned darkly seaward.

Then like a castaway on an interrupted journey, an immensity
of lost steel islanded the channel, hung there in a weight of blue,
shut away my sun. Perhaps it was the ship's aching lines, retraction,

loosening, how it slowly decomposed, perhaps it was its cold void,
the way it held its noise within that made me fear. I swear I saw
his whiteness loom against the glass, a fist, my indoor sea sinking.

But then it was the first day, only 24 hours after he'd left.

Hush.

I love this first hour when Norfolk light seeps red

and all the slight capillaries of the Quiet Lanes

slip from gloam to flush, while up over Trimingham

tattoos of sea-bound birds pin-prick a mantling sky.

Happiness elicits curves, I can undulate these mild berms

in joyful cycled loops all dewy-marked along the marge,

and in a puffery of dandelion time, regress as many years

to ancient drove routes and their hand-scythed rakes of hay

through poppy blood and campion fire. Quakes of earth

scurry vole and shrew, and as I wheel, high grass is ruched

with purring bees. Quiet Lanes. Let me unknow the far-off rush,

just keep this broider of close bird-song and my dawn-sky meandering.

(Norfolk was the first county to introduce Quiet Lanes.
They are 36 miles of clearly sign-posted rural lanes with little traffic,
perfect for cyclists and walkers, and occupy a triangle of North East
Norfolk)

Mundesley. A Passing.

This is where the living wait.
forget the city's distant cubes and soarings,
only our old local now, on a cobbled quay,
your boat and a little sun belying absences.
We're ashed from the morning's scattering,
empty of sea. Talk circles your leaving
like a buoy, and we long for certainty of land,
our beer flat and warm as tilled brown fields.
How to explain that hush of listening glass,
a rush of greening light, as if somewhere
the very water of you turns to leaves.

Mundesley. A Passing

In the Spiegeltent.

In Chapelfield Gardens there's sky-high red-plush

witchery going on. Time travel, a velvet *Belle Epoque*.

We're face-flipped in gilded mirrors, an illusion of shadows

through faceted lifts of light. The stage anchors its heart

in taut suspension. Forget gravity, think of balance-poise-ease,

this sudden somersaulting sultriness of hands, bare skin,

slip-hold fistfuls of it. Feel the rakish fire-breathing

sword-swallowing slap-bang swings across the dome

and then those *oooohs* before each drop. Here is magic.

We're funambulists tip-toeing between another world

and now, wonderstruck with the giddiness. Forget the city,

thrumming along unseen with its May-dusk doings, there's

only this, a tented phantasmagoria and six aerial alchemists

turning our night to gold.

(The spectacular and unusual Spiegeltent is one of the Norfolk and Norwich Festival's major venues. The Festival itself dates back to 1772 when fund raising concerts were held in Norwich Cathedral, and these became annual events in 1778.

Now it is a flagship international arts festival for the East of England, and one of the UK's largest multi-art form festivals. It transforms public spaces, city streets, parks, forests, beaches, and takes place each May for 17 days.)

Ode to the Norfolk Five-Crown Pippin.

Your plump syllables slip between my teeth,
dapple of tree-shade, soft plunks of fruit-fall wicketing grass,
all crunch and roll like cricket balls on Sunday green.
My innocent red-flush-on-the-sunny-side, original-sin tempter,
the smooth fleshed skin of you all tittle-tattle wait in grocers' queues,
a mime of roundness in paper bags, supple buttocky promises
of tart and sweet. You fill my palm, ove, egg, nipple-tassle stalk,
your peel coils down in one long blushing strip before honeyed
oozles of laze-time afternoons and trickle pulpiness.
You pare me to my core as if my age is nothing more
than a distanced *when*, some crisp remembered otherness.
How you seed me in your ancient roots, espaliered walls flint-flowering,
ribbons of sward, kirtles doffed. Oh Pippin, oh apple of my Norfolk eye.

Papermaker

Water-logged with aspen, larch and fir, he takes cream pulp,

settles it down sweet as curds, paddles a long dark

oar across and rests. A quiet surface of page shores up

along the frame and ferries his thoughts to monasteries,

 a meditative marsh of birds, her wading thighs like gleaming carp.

He can almost hear a fishering of bells drifting lines across the Broads,

see Ludham floating, hardly moored to any land-locked thing.

Rimed, his hands hang parchment white, salted,

drying this absence of her. She has nearly gone,

only a shoal of books and bags, bones of little things are left,

her waiting shoes bask delicate as minnows. He's watermarked,

hold him to light, see how the press of her is printed through him.

Papermaker

*'Don't think the garden loses its ecstasy in winter, it's quiet
but the roots are down there riotous' Rumi*

It Will Happen by Chance

that elusive epiphany. A stranger's palms, conched around cup or book

one café morning, will recall to me others with their sudden

curved rapture. It'll happen when I'm autumning through scuffs of yellow

leaves, scrag end of days and plate-glass skies leaning heavy. A swifting

bright will pick out among Holt's trees, wish-bones of old places where I

loved the first or last with him and him and him. It'll startle in a pub's dark

corner flaring with disremembered laughter, or by that pegged jacket its

wooling still warm with lost arms. Some days wild hazel hedges will

shoulder me close like longing suitors down lust-forgotten lanes and a

flushed treacle-taste of skin will surprise my tongue once more. It will

happen when tumbled fruit-fall drifts with humming heat, sedgy midge-

shade pools full of voices surfacing, lapsed desires treading water, and I'll

gasp this in-between. All is in light's wing, I'm neither here nor there, time

and people dovetail fitfully. It'll happen, happen by chance.

Missing.

Once I saw two red deer, flanks so close, running to our Norfolk Sea straight as a die, no tracks back, hooved sand to surf.

Touch. Once I read that a poppy calyx learns insect wings, each coveted beat memorised for more.

Touch. Once I heard that Felbrigg songbirds throng by winter starlight, oh we have lost such mystical intimacy.

Touch. I sit here by an open window, a collage of lockdown sound seeping in from streets, wondering how hot asphalt feels beneath my feet now.

Touch. like my childhood run from promenade to Cromer sand, hopping squirm-toed quick, tar prints on our towels, traces.

Touch. How water lipped my teenage thighs in some preordained way.

Touch. How my blind grandad tapped, tapped flat-fingered from room to room, and his smooth knowing kettle waiting.

Touch. When all this is over, when my door opens and the infinite possibilities of North Sea light flood in, I'll learn |*Touch* once more dear heart. I will try to go slowly so as not to lose anyone. try to be still.

'the vain errand of a dream' John Chapman

The Pedlar's Dog on Swaffham Church Pew.

I'm carved from that time of meandering byways,

of trinkets and gee-gaws on star-puddled nights.

Pothering markets that hoof-clomped and chin-wagged

where *troshels* were white with the scrub of day's niff.

When John's moon tinkered voices it led to illusions

and his apple-tree spading gave not bones but new gold.

Whet your hand on my flank as I sniff bygone seasons,

how lives ripened till death under slow circling skies.

Look how hurtling landscapes have now lost their quiet

journeys, people and places falling stonily away. Do chill

glints of fool's-gold not bury your present, do their coursing

and hounding not have you as the prey? Reflect on the lasting

of sweet countryside light, a pause in its slant as you sit here

today. I'm a memory in oak polished with palming, a simple

wisdom of dog for your tight-tethered age.

(troshel – Norfolk dialect for doorstep)

John Chapman, a tinker from Swaffham in the 15ᵗʰ century, heard a voice night after night, saying that if he went to London Bridge he would have good news. After fruitless days, a man asked him what he wanted and he told him of his dream. The man said that he too dreamt, but of a place called Swaffham with an apple tree at the back of a house, and underneath it was a pot of gold, but he wasn't going to believe in anything so silly. John hurried home, and dug up the pot of gold in his own garden. He became a benefactor of Swaffham Church, and he, his wife and the dog that accompanied him everywhere, are carved on pew finials.

PYO at Wiverton Hall

a light tumble of artichokes, wanton globes,
wait to be stripped skin-bare in my kindly lap.
How blades will slice through these marbled
leaves with luscious ease, sap spilling bloodless
white, hearts hollowed with a lover's deft precision.
These little murders we enact when gripping
vegetable knives, an expiration of some inner
darker fact. Simple potatoes, sloughed skins,
wrinkled cabbage, pared, julienned, shredded.
A barbarous ritual, calculated cookery perhaps,
but understand dear love, that when I harvest news
you've bedded someone else, I line these carrots up
and cut.

Drowned Out.

I'm concentrating on a thin crack in your blue-rimmed bowl,
and the sink is a pool-within-a-pool of suds and souring milk.

You're caught somewhere in the cross-hairs of my vision,
dark and heavy liked the rain-hammered garden, telling me

someone's broken the front gate again, your fists a clench of nails.
It's strange the way light travels clearly through air to water,

how my sopped fingers refract obliquely, as if no longer mine.
I remember it's Tuesday and I must put morning out with the bins,

that there's a pipe-burst on Drayton High Road, all those soiled wakes
of cars slopping walls. Upstairs, the bedroom carpet shifts like shoaled

sand around wrecked boats, a jetsam of chattels lies waiting to be raked.
I'm one of those sea-women counting silence on some quay for a trawler

to sail, knowing that everything, each tide now is down to luck and will.
When the door slams I coast the radio, the shipping forecast, a war or two,

how a woman rowing the North Sea notches each oar with hourless days.
Sudden hail shrapnel's my window, I camouflage and watch clouds break.

Thresholds

Whether to leave now while dry evening light threads field and fen
or wait till they come and fence us, knot us round with untold dark.
The door is the weight of my curved hand, a decision too heavy
to close. Frame and wood, drudging hinge. How even clots of sheep
whitening the green seem to be eyeing, cumbersome with waiting.

Men and glinting muskets, look how they gather on the rise, while lords
of land engirdle, hedge and trench our laborious lives. Tight-lipped
brooding draws me to her face, mother knows the debtor's score, the muck
and mire. I swither between fight and here, a hounded hesitation. How our
harried common ground ebbs free and wide, far-off marsh unyoked water.

Flint and shot, all is red and black in that burning tumult up Ketts Heath,
boots and feet make thunder of their own, drumming through city's skies.
I sit upon the step, resolve in doomy grey and cloud, my fingers are arrows,
arm a flex of bow. Whether to stay or leave depends on this desperate theft
of pasture, halted plough, on the hanging weight of our raging open doors.

Historian Julian Cornwall writing about the 1549 Ketts Rebellion.
'they could scarcely doubt that the state had been taken over by a breed
of men whose policy was to rob the poor for the benefit of the rich'

Thresholds

About the Author.

Mary is a translator who has been living in France for many years, but she has strong links to Norfolk through her parents and close family. She has won the Wenlock Prize, Segora Prize, Wirral Prize, the Sentinel Quarterly Competition, the D.M Thomas Poetry on the Lake Competition, the Pen Nib International Poetry Prize, and has been shortlisted several times for the Bridport Prize. Placed and Commended in the Teignmouth, Caterpillar, Prole, Bedford, Buzzwords, The Plough, Yaffle, Cannon Sonnets, Stroud and Spelt Magazine Prizes. Her work has been published by Magma, Antiphon, Obsessed with Pipework, Strix, Smeuse, Clear Poetry, Ekphrastic Review, The Morning Star 21st Century Poetry, among many others. It also appears in several Anthologies such as The Very Best of 52, Mildly Erotic Verse (Emma Press), Samhain (3 Drops from a Cauldron), The Road to Cleveland Pier, A Restricted View from Under the Hedge (Hedgehog Press). Her pamphlet 'Incidentals' is published by 4Word Press.

Acknowledgements.

Most of these poems are unpublished, but others were previously published by The Morning Star, Word Bohemia, Clear Poetry, Visual Verse, Prole, The Phare, and The Fenland Journal.

My grateful thanks above all to Peter Norton, for his art, inspiration, and encouragement, without whom this collection would never have seen the light of day.

Peter's photographic work can be found on the Sublime Norfolk website which explores the stunning County of Norfolk, and its unique beauty. Here his brush sketches interpret and compliment my poems.